LIGHTNING
BOLT
BOOKS™

Give It a Push!
Give It a Pull!
A Look at Forces

Jennifer Boothroyd

Lerner Publications
Minneapolis

To my dear friend Ava—who is a force to be reckoned with
—J.B.

Lerner Publications Company
A division of Lerner Publishing Group, Inc.
241 First Avenue North
Minneapolis, MN 55401 USA

For reading levels and more information, look up this title at www.lernerbooks.com.

Library of Congress Cataloging-in-Publication Data

Boothroyd, Jennifer, 1972-
    Give It a Push! Give It a Pull!: A Look at Forces / by Jennifer Boothroyd.
      p.   cm. — (Lightning bolt books™—Exploring Physical Science)
    Includes index.
    ISBN 978–0–7613–5431–4 (lib. bdg. : alk. paper)
    ISBN 978–0–7613–6297–5 (EB pdf)
    1. Force and energy—Juvenile literature. 2. Motion—Juvenile literature. 3. Friction—Juvenile literature. I. Title.
    QC73.4.B66 2011
    531'.6—dc22   2009037698

Manufactured in the United States of America
13-46090-10986-5/24/2018

Contents

Pushes and Pulls

A force is a push or a pull. Forces are always with you. They are all around you.

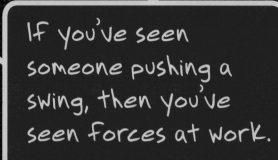

If you've seen someone pushing a swing, then you've seen forces at work.

Most of the time, you can see the cause of a force. A person pushes a swing. A truck pulls a boat.

When a truck pulls a boat, you see the truck doing the pulling.

Sometimes the cause of a force is invisible.

Wind pushes leaves across a sidewalk.

The wind is invisible.

Gravity pulls a paper airplane down. Magnetism holds magnets against a fridge.

Magnetism pulls this magnet against the fridge. Magnetism is invisible.

Putting Things in Motion

Forces put things in motion. Pushing the pedal makes the tire spin.

Pulling a wagon
makes it roll.

Pushing and pulling your pencil lets you write your name.

Thanks to forces, you can write on a sheet of paper.

A push moves something away from the force.

This toy car moves away from the boy when he pushes it.

A pull moves something closer to the force.

This rope moves closer to the girl when she pulls it.

Stronger forces can make things move farther.

You can throw a ball across the yard with a strong push.

A strong force will make a football sail far away from you.

A gentle force makes things move only a little. A little push gets this boat on its way.

A gentle force will make a toy boat move a short distance from you.

An object's weight can change the force needed to move it.

It takes a lot of force to pick up a heavy suitcase.

It takes only a little force to lift a light feather.

Direction and Speed

A force makes something move in one direction. Another force can change it. A pitcher throws a ball to the batter.

The batter hits the ball.
The ball flies in a
different direction.

Forces change the speed of things. A strong force can make something move quickly.

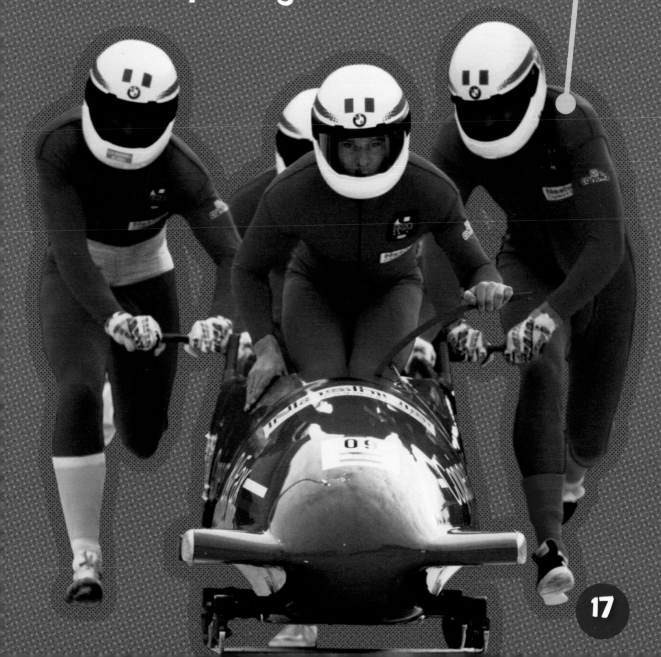

A strong push of a bobsled makes the sled move very quickly.

A strong wind makes a sailboat race across the lake. A hard pull on the wheels makes a wheelchair speed along the ground.

This racer pulls hard on the wheels of his special wheelchair so he can win the race!

Forces make things stop moving. A brick wall will stop a ball. The wall has a lot of force. It pushes against the ball.

A tennis ball will stop moving forward when it hits a brick wall.

A glass window may not stop a ball. Glass pushes against a ball too. But the ball pushes even harder than the glass.

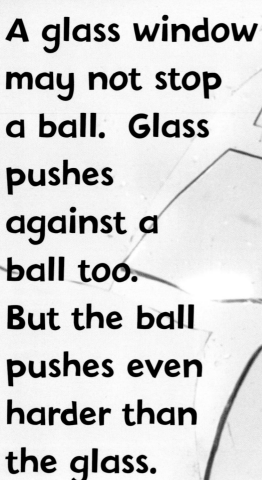

A glass window has less force than a brick wall, so a ball may sail right through it. That's bad news for whoever hit the ball!

An object's weight can give an idea of the force needed to stop it. It takes a lot of force to stop a train.

Only something with a huge amount of force could make this great big train stop.

It takes a little force to stop a Ping-Pong ball.

A small paddle is enough to stop a tiny Ping-Pong ball.

Friction

Friction is a force that slows things down or makes them stop. Rubbing your feet on the ground creates friction. The friction makes a swing stop.

Friction is created when an object—such as your feet—rubs against another object—such as the ground.

Friction from the brakes makes your bike stop.

When you hit the brakes on your bike, the brakes rub against the wheels.

A smooth surface makes less friction. You can slide easily on ice but not on grass.

Changing Shape

Forces change the shape of things. It takes a push to flatten dough. It takes a pull to stretch it out.

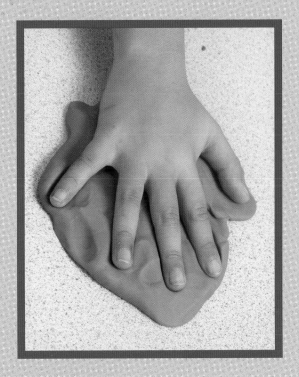

The force of the wind
bends the trees.
Twisting a balloon
changes its shape.

Someone made this
balloon animal by pulling
on and twisting a balloon.

Forces are everywhere. They help us eat, work, and play. Nothing would happen without forces!

Activity

Ball Toss Game

You will need to use different amounts of force to play this game.

What you need:

3 yardsticks

3 5-gallon (20-liter) buckets

a Ping-Pong ball

a golf ball

a softball

a soccer ball

What you do:

1. Place the yardsticks on the ground to make a capital letter *L*. Use two sticks for the side and one for the bottom.

2. Place the buckets next to the long side inside the L shape. Space the buckets 12 inches (30 centimeters) apart.

3. Stand with your toes behind the bottom of the L shape.

4. Toss the Ping-Pong ball into the closest bucket. Then toss it into the second and last buckets.

5. Think about which toss took more force.

6. Repeat the tosses with each type of ball. Which toss needed the most force? Which ball needed the most force to move?

Glossary

direction: the way that someone or something is moving

force: a push or a pull

friction: a force that slows things down or makes them stop. Rubbing creates friction.

gravity: a force that pulls things down toward the surface of Earth

magnetism: a force that attracts certain metals to magnets

motion: movement

speed: the rate at which something moves

weight: the measure of how heavy a person or thing is

Further Reading

BBC Schools Science Clips: Pushes and Pulls
http://www.bbc.co.uk/schools/scienceclips/ages/5_6/
pushes_pulls.shtml

Bradley, Kimberly Brubaker. *Forces Make Things Move.* New York: HarperCollins, 2005.

Forces
http://www.zephyrus.co.uk/forces1.html

Nelson, Robin. *Push and Pull.* Minneapolis: Lerner Publications Company, 2004.

Park World Plot
http://www.engineeringinteract
.org/resources/parkworldplot.htm

Royston, Angela. *Looking at Forces and Motion: How Do Things Move?* Berkeley Heights, NJ: Enslow Publishers, 2008.

Index

Photo Acknowledgments

The images in this book are used with the permission of: © Kane Skennar/Digital Vision/Getty Images, p. 2; © iStockphoto.com/Ann Marie Kurtz, p. 4; © Jason Lindsey/Alamy, p. 5; © Michael Blann/Digital Vision/Getty Images, p. 6; © Todd Strand/Independent Picture Service, pp. 7, 25 (both), 28 (soccer ball and buckets), 29 (all); © age fotostock/SuperStock, p. 8; © H. Mark Weidman Photography/Alamy, p. 9; © Jose Manuel Gelpi Diaz/Dreamstime.com, p. 10; © Fancy/Photolibrary, p. 11 (left); © Mark Mann/Digital Vision/Getty Images, p. 11 (right); © David Madison/Photographer's Choice/Getty Images, p. 12; © Dorling Kindersley/Getty Images, p. 13; © Hill Creek Pictures/UpperCut Images/Getty Images, p. 14 (top); © ZenShui/Sigrid Olsson/PhotoAlto Agency RF Collections/Getty Images, p. 14 (bottom); © iStockphoto.com/Jim Kolaczko, p. 15; © iStockphoto.com/Rob Friedman, p. 16; © Action Plus/Stone/Getty Images, p. 17; © Fabrice Coffrini/AFP/Getty Images, p. 18; © Marcelo Santos/The Image Bank/Getty Images, p. 19; © Tom Branch/Photo Researchers, Inc., p. 20; © iStockphoto.com/Simon Smith, p. 21 (left); © mylife photos/Alamy, p. 21 (right); © iStockphoto.com/Slobo Mitic, p. 22; © SW Productions/Photodisc/Getty Images, p. 23; © Viviolsen/Dreamstime.com, p. 24; © iStockphoto.com/Nikita Rogul, p. 26; © Digital Vision/Getty Images, p. 27; © Nikkytok/Dreamstime.com, p. 28 (golf ball); © iStockphoto.com/Stephanie Perez, p. 28 (softball); © Vitaly Yamzin/Dreamstime.com, p. 28 (Ping-Pong ball); © Jose Luis Pelaez/The Image Bank/Getty Images, pp. 30-31.

Front Cover: © Fancy/Photolibrary (top), © Peter Cade/Iconica/Getty Images (bottom).